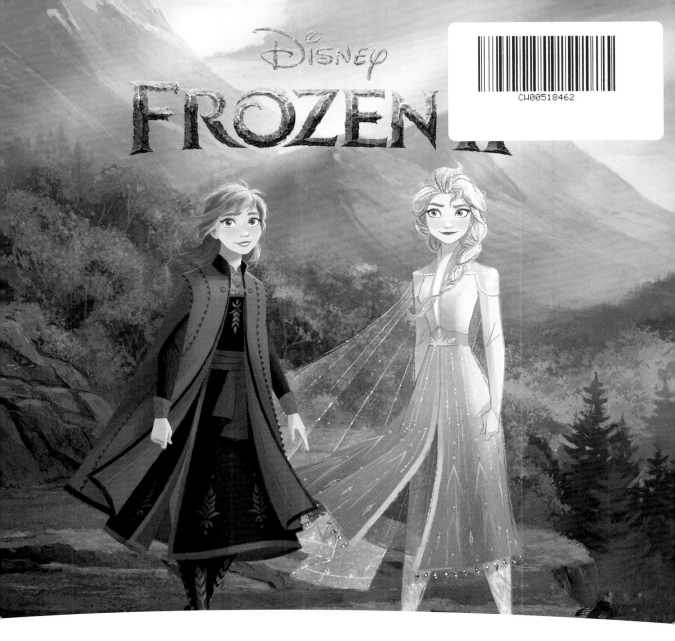

Level 3

Re-told by: Nicola Schofield
Series Editor: Rachel Wilson

Pearson Education Limited
KAO Two
KAO Park, Harlow,
Essex, CMI7 9NA, England
and Associated Companies throughout the world.

ISBN: 978-1-2923-4679-3

This edition first published by Pearson Education Ltd 2021

1 3 5 7 9 10 8 6 4 2

Set in Heinemann Roman Special, 14pt/23pt
Printed by Neografia, Slovakia

Published by Pearson Education Limited

Acknowledgments
123RF.com: Boyan Dimitrov 22
Alamy Stock Photo: Helena Ryan 22
Getty Images: aniszewski 23, Aumphotography 26-27, Martin Ruegner 23, Ulga 24
Shutterstock.com: Andrea Leone 24, Juancat 27

For a complete list of the titles available in the Pearson English Readers series, visit www.pearsonenglishreaders.com.

Alternatively, write to your local Pearson Education office or to Pearson English Readers Marketing Department, Pearson Education, KAO Two, KAO Park, Harlow, Essex, CMI7 9NA

In This Book

Elsa
Queen of Arendelle

Anna
Elsa's sister and Princess of Arendelle

Olaf
A magic snowman

Kristoff
Anna's boyfriend

Sven the Reindeer
Kristoff's friend

Grand Pabbie the Troll
Elsa's friend

Before You Read

Introduction

King Agnarr tells Elsa and Anna a story about a place called the Enchanted Forest. Years later, Elsa hears a voice and she follows it. Anna, Kristoff, Sven, and Olaf go with her. But what is it? Where's it coming from? Can they find the answers?

Activities

1 **Choose the words to complete the sentences.**

> appeared   fight   ground   past   save   voice

1 She has a beautiful singing ....

2 There's snow on the ....

3 In the .... , people lived in villages.

4 Suddenly, the horse .... from behind the tree.

5 Please .... my sister—she's falling!

6 Don't .... with your brother! It's not kind.

2 **Look at the picture and answer the questions.**

1 Who's in the picture?

2 Where do you think they are?

3 What do you think they're doing?

4 How do you think they're feeling?

King Agnarr of Arendelle loves telling stories to his daughters,
Elsa and Anna. One night, he tells them about the Northuldra.
They live in the Enchanted Forest and they love spirits and
nature. Years before, the Arendellians made a dam for the
Northuldra because they were friends.

But one day, there was a fight between them. Now the
Northuldra can't leave the forest.
The girls have a lot of questions for their parents, but it's time
for bed. Queen Iduna sings a song and the girls go to sleep.

Years later …

One evening, Elsa, Anna, Olaf, Kristoff, and Sven, are playing games in the castle. They're having fun. Suddenly, Elsa stops. There's a voice, but only she can hear it.

"Are you okay?" Anna asks.

"A little … tired," Elsa answers.

Anna follows Elsa to her room. Elsa is wearing their mother's scarf.

"What's wrong?" Anna asks.

"There's this …" but Elsa can't tell Anna about the voice.

She sings to Anna—their mother's song about Ahtohallan. It's a magic river that holds stories of the past. They fall asleep.

Elsa wakes! She hears the voice again. This time, she follows
it outside. Elsa uses her magic. She changes the snow into
beautiful ice shapes. She can see pictures in them.
"Wind, Fire, Water, Earth!" Elsa wakes the spirits of nature.

Back at the castle, Anna sees the same ice shapes. She doesn't understand what's happening. Now ice shapes are falling from the sky. *CRASH!*
There's no water or light. The ground suddenly moves. In Arendelle, people are afraid. They're running from their homes.

Elsa's friend, Grand Pabbie, arrives. "The spirits are angry,"
he says. "Understand the past, then you can save Arendelle."
Elsa feels strong, "I have to go to the Enchanted Forest and
find that voice."

"You're hearing voices?" Kristoff asks.

"Not voices, a voice," Elsa says.

Kristoff and Anna don't like this idea.

"We have to come with you!" Anna says.

"I can stay and help the people of Arendelle," Grand Pabbie
says kindly.

Early the next morning, Elsa, Anna, Kristoff, Olaf, and Sven
go north.

The next day, they arrive at a wall of mist.

"I hear the voice!" Elsa shouts.

They run through the mist. Elsa stops in front of four large rocks. She remembers these pictures of the spirits. The same ones were on the ice shapes.

Suddenly, the Wind Spirit pushes the friends into the forest.
Elsa uses her magic to stop the wind. Snow from her hands
makes ice shapes appear. They see their young father and
a Northuldra girl in the ice. She's saving him.
Who *is* she?

There's a noise—Northuldra people appear from the trees.
Then Arendellians appear! They fight. Elsa uses her magic,
and she stops the fight. The people are surprised.
"I am Queen of Arendelle," Elsa says, "I want to help you
leave the forest."

Suddenly, a ball of fire flies at them. The Fire Spirit! The people run. Elsa uses her magic and stops the spirit. A small, friendly animal appears.

Anna was afraid of the fire. Elsa puts their mother's scarf around her sister.

"That's a Northuldra scarf," a man says. Now the sisters understand—the Northuldra girl in the ice was their mother!

There are pictures of the spirits on the scarf. There's also a fifth spirit— a bridge between the magic of nature and people. They have to find that bridge.

They go north and see a boat.

Inside the boat, they find a map. There's a river called
Ahtohallan. It's the river from their mother's song—it holds
stories of the past.
Elsa has to find Ahtohallan, but not with Anna. It's very
dangerous.

Elsa arrives at the Dark Sea.
She makes ice on the water.
But it's no good! She goes
underwater.
Suddenly, there's a water horse—
it's the Water Spirit! It's angry and
they fight. Elsa jumps on the horse
and they ride across the Dark Sea.

Elsa arrives at Ahtohallan—the magic river is a glacier!
The voice is calling her.

Suddenly, pictures of her mother and her grandfather, King
Runeard of Arendelle, appear on the walls of ice.
It's true—Ahtohallan *does* hold stories of the past!

Her grandfather hated the Northuldra. He didn't make the dam because they were friends. He wanted to *hurt* them!
Elsa uses her magic. The ice shows Anna what happened.
Anna shouts, "The dam has to fall!"
She wants to make things right again.

Her idea is to use the Earth Spirit.

"Wake up!" Anna shouts at the Earth Giants.

They become angrier and angrier. She runs to the dam. The Earth Giants throw things at Anna and the dam starts to fall. Her idea is dangerous, but it's working!

Anna's afraid. Now all the water from the dam is running straight to Arendelle! But Elsa appears and makes a wall of ice.
Suddenly, it's sunny again in the Enchanted Forest. The Northuldra can leave, and they can smile again.

Anna and Elsa are happy again. They understand the true story of the past. With their friends' help, they saved Arendelle. Anna is now Queen Anna, and Elsa is the fifth spirit. She is the bridge between the magic of nature and people; between the Northuldra and the Arendellians.

After You Read

1 **Match the spirits to the pictures.**

1 Water Spirit **2** Earth Spirit **3** Fire Spirit **4** Wind Spirit

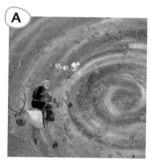
A

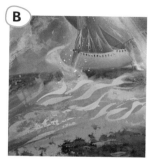
B

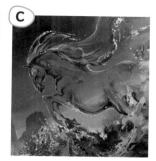
C

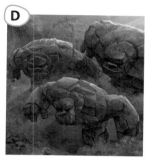
D

2 **Match the names to the sentences.**

Grand Pabbie Elsa Anna Kristoff

1 "Wind, Earth, Water, Fire!"
2 "The spirits are angry."
3 "You're hearing voices?"
4 "The dam has to fall!"

3 **Put the story into the correct order.**

a Elsa goes to the Dark Sea.
b In the castle, Elsa hears a voice.
c The friends go north to the Enchanted Forest.
d The Northuldra are happy again and can leave the forest.
e Anna shouts and the dam falls.

Picture Dictionary

dam

earth

fire

glacier

ice

map

mist

nature

river

scarf

snow

spirits

Phonics

Say the sounds. Read the words.

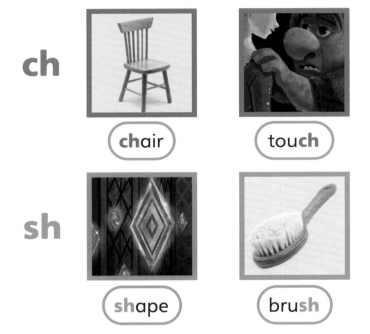

ch

chair

touch

sh

shape

brush

Say the rhyme.

Elsa shows Anna
The shapes in the snow.
She touches them,
She watches them,
And Anna shouts, "Oh!"

Values

Keep going.

Look! It's from Elsa! Our grandfather was a bad man.

Oh no, Anna. What's happening to me?

Olaf, don't go!

I'm sorry.

I can't do this without Elsa and Olaf!

No, I'm okay. I can be strong. I have to do the right thing!

Find Out

What do you know about glaciers?

Glaciers are very big rivers of ice. They're moving slowly all the time. Some glaciers move 25 centimeters a day. Some glaciers move 30 meters a day. That's a big difference. But we can't see this with our eyes. There are a lot of glaciers in Antarctica, Greenland and Alaska. But you can find them in cold places all over the world.

percent (%) out of 100; 70% of the Earth is water, 30% is land
thousand the number 1,000
centimeter (cm) / meter (m) 100 centimeters = 1 meter
kilometer (km) 1,000 meters = 1 kilometer

Fast Facts

- Some glacier ice is more than a hundred thousand (100,000) years old.

- Lambert Glacier, in Antarctica, is 400 kilometers long.

- 69 percent of water comes from glaciers. Perhaps there's some water from a glacier in your glass right now …

- An iceberg is ice from a glacier.

an iceberg in Antarctica